ADDRESS BOOK

This Book Belongs to:

Name: ....

Phone: ....

Email: ....

A

Name	
Address	
Home	Mobile
Work	Email
Anniversary	Birthday
Notes	

Name	
Address	
Home	Mobile
Work	Email
Anniversary	Birthday
Notes	

Name	
Address	
Home	Mobile
Work	Email
Anniversary	Birthday
Notes	

Name

Address

Home | Mobile

Work | Email

Anniversary | Birthday

Notes

Name

Address

Home | Mobile

Work | Email

Anniversary | Birthday

Notes

Name

Address

Home | Mobile

Work | Email

Anniversary | Birthday

Notes

A

Name	
Address	

Home	Mobile
Work	Email
Anniversary	Birthday
Notes	

Name	
Address	

Home	Mobile
Work	Email
Anniversary	Birthday
Notes	

Name	
Address	

Home	Mobile
Work	Email
Anniversary	Birthday
Notes	

A

Name	
Address	

Home	Mobile
Work	Email
Anniversary	Birthday
Notes	

Name	
Address	

Home	Mobile
Work	Email
Anniversary	Birthday
Notes	

Name	
Address	

Home	Mobile
Work	Email
Anniversary	Birthday
Notes	

B

Name

Address

Home	Mobile
Work	Email
Anniversary	Birthday
Notes	

Name

Address

Home	Mobile
Work	Email
Anniversary	Birthday
Notes	

Name

Address

Home	Mobile
Work	Email
Anniversary	Birthday
Notes	

B

Name

Address

Home	Mobile
Work	Email
Anniversary	Birthday
Notes	

Name

Address

Home	Mobile
Work	Email
Anniversary	Birthday
Notes	

Name

Address

Home	Mobile
Work	Email
Anniversary	Birthday
Notes	

B

Name

Address

Home | Mobile

Work | Email

Anniversary | Birthday

Notes

Name

Address

Home | Mobile

Work | Email

Anniversary | Birthday

Notes

Name

Address

Home | Mobile

Work | Email

Anniversary | Birthday

Notes

B

Name

Address

Home   Mobile

Work   Email

Anniversary   Birthday

Notes

Name

Address

Home   Mobile

Work   Email

Anniversary   Birthday

Notes

Name

Address

Home   Mobile

Work   Email

Anniversary   Birthday

Notes

C

Name

Address

Home	Mobile
Work	Email
Anniversary	Birthday

Notes

Name

Address

Home	Mobile
Work	Email
Anniversary	Birthday

Notes

Name

Address

Home	Mobile
Work	Email
Anniversary	Birthday

Notes

Name

Address

Home   Mobile

Work   Email

Anniversary   Birthday

Notes

Name

Address

Home   Mobile

Work   Email

Anniversary   Birthday

Notes

Name

Address

Home   Mobile

Work   Email

Anniversary   Birthday

Notes

C

Name

Address

Home	Mobile
Work	Email
Anniversary	Birthday

Notes

Name

Address

Home	Mobile
Work	Email
Anniversary	Birthday

Notes

Name

Address

Home	Mobile
Work	Email
Anniversary	Birthday

Notes

C

Name

Address

Home   Mobile

Work   Email

Anniversary   Birthday

Notes

Name

Address

Home   Mobile

Work   Email

Anniversary   Birthday

Notes

Name

Address

Home   Mobile

Work   Email

Anniversary   Birthday

Notes

D

Name

Address

Home | Mobile

Work | Email

Anniversary | Birthday

Notes

Name

Address

Home | Mobile

Work | Email

Anniversary | Birthday

Notes

Name

Address

Home | Mobile

Work | Email

Anniversary | Birthday

Notes

D

Name

Address

Home	Mobile
Work	Email
Anniversary	Birthday

Notes

Name

Address

Home	Mobile
Work	Email
Anniversary	Birthday

Notes

Name

Address

Home	Mobile
Work	Email
Anniversary	Birthday

Notes

Name

Address

Home   Mobile

Work   Email

Anniversary   Birthday

Notes

Name

Address

Home   Mobile

Work   Email

Anniversary   Birthday

Notes

Name

Address

Home   Mobile

Work   Email

Anniversary   Birthday

Notes

Name

Address

Home   Mobile

Work   Email

Anniversary   Birthday

Notes

Name

Address

Home   Mobile

Work   Email

Anniversary   Birthday

Notes

Name

Address

Home   Mobile

Work   Email

Anniversary   Birthday

Notes

E

Name

Address

Home   Mobile

Work   Email

Anniversary   Birthday

Notes

Name

Address

Home   Mobile

Work   Email

Anniversary   Birthday

Notes

Name

Address

Home   Mobile

Work   Email

Anniversary   Birthday

Notes

Name

Address

Home   Mobile

Work   Email

Anniversary   Birthday

Notes

Name

Address

Home   Mobile

Work   Email

Anniversary   Birthday

Notes

Name

Address

Home   Mobile

Work   Email

Anniversary   Birthday

Notes

E

Name

Address

Home	Mobile
Work	Email
Anniversary	Birthday
Notes	

Name

Address

Home	Mobile
Work	Email
Anniversary	Birthday
Notes	

Name

Address

Home	Mobile
Work	Email
Anniversary	Birthday
Notes	

Name

Address

Home	Mobile
Work	Email
Anniversary	Birthday
Notes	

Name

Address

Home	Mobile
Work	Email
Anniversary	Birthday
Notes	

Name

Address

Home	Mobile
Work	Email
Anniversary	Birthday
Notes	

F

Name

Address

Home	Mobile
Work	Email
Anniversary	Birthday

Notes

Name

Address

Home	Mobile
Work	Email
Anniversary	Birthday

Notes

Name

Address

Home	Mobile
Work	Email
Anniversary	Birthday

Notes

F

Name

Address

Home   Mobile

Work   Email

Anniversary   Birthday

Notes

Name

Address

Home   Mobile

Work   Email

Anniversary   Birthday

Notes

Name

Address

Home   Mobile

Work   Email

Anniversary   Birthday

Notes

F

Name

Address

Home	Mobile
Work	Email
Anniversary	Birthday
Notes	

Name

Address

Home	Mobile
Work	Email
Anniversary	Birthday
Notes	

Name

Address

Home	Mobile
Work	Email
Anniversary	Birthday
Notes	

Name

Address

Home   Mobile

Work   Email

Anniversary   Birthday

Notes

Name

Address

Home   Mobile

Work   Email

Anniversary   Birthday

Notes

Name

Address

Home   Mobile

Work   Email

Anniversary   Birthday

Notes

G

Name

Address

Home | Mobile

Work | Email

Anniversary | Birthday

Notes

Name

Address

Home | Mobile

Work | Email

Anniversary | Birthday

Notes

Name

Address

Home | Mobile

Work | Email

Anniversary | Birthday

Notes

G

Name

Address

Home   Mobile

Work   Email

Anniversary   Birthday

Notes

Name

Address

Home   Mobile

Work   Email

Anniversary   Birthday

Notes

Name

Address

Home   Mobile

Work   Email

Anniversary   Birthday

Notes

G

Name	
Address	

Home	Mobile
Work	Email
Anniversary	Birthday
Notes	

Name	
Address	

Home	Mobile
Work	Email
Anniversary	Birthday
Notes	

Name	
Address	

Home	Mobile
Work	Email
Anniversary	Birthday
Notes	

G

Name

Address

Home   Mobile

Work   Email

Anniversary   Birthday

Notes

Name

Address

Home   Mobile

Work   Email

Anniversary   Birthday

Notes

Name

Address

Home   Mobile

Work   Email

Anniversary   Birthday

Notes

Name	
Address	
Home	Mobile
Work	Email
Anniversary	Birthday
Notes	

Name	
Address	
Home	Mobile
Work	Email
Anniversary	Birthday
Notes	

Name	
Address	
Home	Mobile
Work	Email
Anniversary	Birthday
Notes	

Name

Address

Home   Mobile

Work   Email

Anniversary   Birthday

Notes

Name

Address

Home   Mobile

Work   Email

Anniversary   Birthday

Notes

Name

Address

Home   Mobile

Work   Email

Anniversary   Birthday

Notes

H

Name	
Address	

Home	Mobile
Work	Email
Anniversary	Birthday
Notes	

Name	
Address	

Home	Mobile
Work	Email
Anniversary	Birthday
Notes	

Name	
Address	

Home	Mobile
Work	Email
Anniversary	Birthday
Notes	

H

Name

Address

Home	Mobile
Work	Email
Anniversary	Birthday
Notes	

Name

Address

Home	Mobile
Work	Email
Anniversary	Birthday
Notes	

Name

Address

Home	Mobile
Work	Email
Anniversary	Birthday
Notes	

I

Name

Address

Home | Mobile
Work | Email
Anniversary | Birthday
Notes

Name

Address

Home | Mobile
Work | Email
Anniversary | Birthday
Notes

Name

Address

Home | Mobile
Work | Email
Anniversary | Birthday
Notes

Name

Address

Home   Mobile

Work   Email

Anniversary   Birthday

Notes

Name

Address

Home   Mobile

Work   Email

Anniversary   Birthday

Notes

Name

Address

Home   Mobile

Work   Email

Anniversary   Birthday

Notes

I

Name	
Address	

Home	Mobile
Work	Email
Anniversary	Birthday
Notes	

Name	
Address	

Home	Mobile
Work	Email
Anniversary	Birthday
Notes	

Name	
Address	

Home	Mobile
Work	Email
Anniversary	Birthday
Notes	

Name

Address

Home   Mobile

Work   Email

Anniversary   Birthday

Notes

Name

Address

Home   Mobile

Work   Email

Anniversary   Birthday

Notes

Name

Address

Home   Mobile

Work   Email

Anniversary   Birthday

Notes

J

Name

Address

Home   Mobile

Work   Email

Anniversary   Birthday

Notes

Name

Address

Home   Mobile

Work   Email

Anniversary   Birthday

Notes

Name

Address

Home   Mobile

Work   Email

Anniversary   Birthday

Notes

J

Name	
Address	

Home	Mobile
Work	Email
Anniversary	Birthday
Notes	

Name	
Address	

Home	Mobile
Work	Email
Anniversary	Birthday
Notes	

Name	
Address	

Home	Mobile
Work	Email
Anniversary	Birthday
Notes	

J

Name

Address

Home	Mobile
Work	Email
Anniversary	Birthday
Notes	

Name

Address

Home	Mobile
Work	Email
Anniversary	Birthday
Notes	

Name

Address

Home	Mobile
Work	Email
Anniversary	Birthday
Notes	

J

Name	
Address	
Home	Mobile
Work	Email
Anniversary	Birthday
Notes	

Name	
Address	
Home	Mobile
Work	Email
Anniversary	Birthday
Notes	

Name	
Address	
Home	Mobile
Work	Email
Anniversary	Birthday
Notes	

K

Name

Address

Home   Mobile

Work   Email

Anniversary   Birthday

Notes

Name

Address

Home   Mobile

Work   Email

Anniversary   Birthday

Notes

Name

Address

Home   Mobile

Work   Email

Anniversary   Birthday

Notes

Name	
Address	
Home	Mobile
Work	Email
Anniversary	Birthday
Notes	

Name	
Address	
Home	Mobile
Work	Email
Anniversary	Birthday
Notes	

Name	
Address	
Home	Mobile
Work	Email
Anniversary	Birthday
Notes	

Name

Address

Home   Mobile

Work   Email

Anniversary   Birthday

Notes

Name

Address

Home   Mobile

Work   Email

Anniversary   Birthday

Notes

Name

Address

Home   Mobile

Work   Email

Anniversary   Birthday

Notes

K

Name	
Address	

Home	Mobile
Work	Email
Anniversary	Birthday
Notes	

Name	
Address	

Home	Mobile
Work	Email
Anniversary	Birthday
Notes	

Name	
Address	

Home	Mobile
Work	Email
Anniversary	Birthday
Notes	

L

Name	
Address	

Home	Mobile
Work	Email
Anniversary	Birthday
Notes	

Name	
Address	

Home	Mobile
Work	Email
Anniversary	Birthday
Notes	

Name	
Address	

Home	Mobile
Work	Email
Anniversary	Birthday
Notes	

Name

Address

Home	Mobile
Work	Email
Anniversary	Birthday
Notes	

Name

Address

Home	Mobile
Work	Email
Anniversary	Birthday
Notes	

Name

Address

Home	Mobile
Work	Email
Anniversary	Birthday
Notes	

L

Name

Address

Home	Mobile
Work	Email
Anniversary	Birthday

Notes

Name

Address

Home	Mobile
Work	Email
Anniversary	Birthday

Notes

Name

Address

Home	Mobile
Work	Email
Anniversary	Birthday

Notes

L

Name

Address

Home | Mobile
Work | Email
Anniversary | Birthday

Notes

Name

Address

Home | Mobile
Work | Email
Anniversary | Birthday

Notes

Name

Address

Home | Mobile
Work | Email
Anniversary | Birthday

Notes

Name

Address

Home   Mobile

Work   Email

Anniversary   Birthday

Notes

Name

Address

Home   Mobile

Work   Email

Anniversary   Birthday

Notes

Name

Address

Home   Mobile

Work   Email

Anniversary   Birthday

Notes

Name

Address

Home   Mobile

Work   Email

Anniversary   Birthday

Notes

Name

Address

Home   Mobile

Work   Email

Anniversary   Birthday

Notes

Name

Address

Home   Mobile

Work   Email

Anniversary   Birthday

Notes

M

Name	
Address	

Home	Mobile
Work	Email
Anniversary	Birthday
Notes	

Name	
Address	

Home	Mobile
Work	Email
Anniversary	Birthday
Notes	

Name	
Address	

Home	Mobile
Work	Email
Anniversary	Birthday
Notes	

Name

Address

Home   Mobile

Work   Email

Anniversary   Birthday

Notes

Name

Address

Home   Mobile

Work   Email

Anniversary   Birthday

Notes

Name

Address

Home   Mobile

Work   Email

Anniversary   Birthday

Notes

N

Name

Address

Home | Mobile
Work | Email
Anniversary | Birthday
Notes

Name

Address

Home | Mobile
Work | Email
Anniversary | Birthday
Notes

Name

Address

Home | Mobile
Work | Email
Anniversary | Birthday
Notes

N

Name

Address

Home | Mobile

Work | Email

Anniversary | Birthday

Notes

Name

Address

Home | Mobile

Work | Email

Anniversary | Birthday

Notes

Name

Address

Home | Mobile

Work | Email

Anniversary | Birthday

Notes

N

Name

Address

Home	Mobile
Work	Email
Anniversary	Birthday
Notes	

Name

Address

Home	Mobile
Work	Email
Anniversary	Birthday
Notes	

Name

Address

Home	Mobile
Work	Email
Anniversary	Birthday
Notes	

Name

Address

Home	Mobile
Work	Email
Anniversary	Birthday
Notes	

Name

Address

Home	Mobile
Work	Email
Anniversary	Birthday
Notes	

Name

Address

Home	Mobile
Work	Email
Anniversary	Birthday
Notes	

O

Name

Address

Home | Mobile

Work | Email

Anniversary | Birthday

Notes

Name

Address

Home | Mobile

Work | Email

Anniversary | Birthday

Notes

Name

Address

Home | Mobile

Work | Email

Anniversary | Birthday

Notes

O

Name

Address

Home   Mobile

Work   Email

Anniversary   Birthday

Notes

Name

Address

Home   Mobile

Work   Email

Anniversary   Birthday

Notes

Name

Address

Home   Mobile

Work   Email

Anniversary   Birthday

Notes

Name	
Address	

Home	Mobile
Work	Email
Anniversary	Birthday
Notes	

Name	
Address	

Home	Mobile
Work	Email
Anniversary	Birthday
Notes	

Name	
Address	

Home	Mobile
Work	Email
Anniversary	Birthday
Notes	

O

Name	
Address	
Home	Mobile
Work	Email
Anniversary	Birthday
Notes	

Name	
Address	
Home	Mobile
Work	Email
Anniversary	Birthday
Notes	

Name	
Address	
Home	Mobile
Work	Email
Anniversary	Birthday
Notes	

Name

Address

Home   Mobile

Work   Email

Anniversary   Birthday

Notes

Name

Address

Home   Mobile

Work   Email

Anniversary   Birthday

Notes

Name

Address

Home   Mobile

Work   Email

Anniversary   Birthday

Notes

P

Name

Address

Home | Mobile

Work | Email

Anniversary | Birthday

Notes

Name

Address

Home | Mobile

Work | Email

Anniversary | Birthday

Notes

Name

Address

Home | Mobile

Work | Email

Anniversary | Birthday

Notes

P

Name	
Address	

Home	Mobile
Work	Email
Anniversary	Birthday
Notes	

Name	
Address	

Home	Mobile
Work	Email
Anniversary	Birthday
Notes	

Name	
Address	

Home	Mobile
Work	Email
Anniversary	Birthday
Notes	

P

Name

Address

Home   Mobile

Work   Email

Anniversary   Birthday

Notes

Name

Address

Home   Mobile

Work   Email

Anniversary   Birthday

Notes

Name

Address

Home   Mobile

Work   Email

Anniversary   Birthday

Notes

Name

Address

Home   Mobile

Work   Email

Anniversary   Birthday

Notes

Name

Address

Home   Mobile

Work   Email

Anniversary   Birthday

Notes

Name

Address

Home   Mobile

Work   Email

Anniversary   Birthday

Notes

Q

Name

Address

Home	Mobile
Work	Email
Anniversary	Birthday
Notes	

Name

Address

Home	Mobile
Work	Email
Anniversary	Birthday
Notes	

Name

Address

Home	Mobile
Work	Email
Anniversary	Birthday
Notes	

Name

Address

Home	Mobile
Work	Email
Anniversary	Birthday
Notes	

Name

Address

Home	Mobile
Work	Email
Anniversary	Birthday
Notes	

Name

Address

Home	Mobile
Work	Email
Anniversary	Birthday
Notes	

Q

Name

Address

Home   Mobile

Work   Email

Anniversary   Birthday

Notes

Name

Address

Home   Mobile

Work   Email

Anniversary   Birthday

Notes

Name

Address

Home   Mobile

Work   Email

Anniversary   Birthday

Notes

Name

Address

Home	Mobile
Work	Email
Anniversary	Birthday
Notes	

Name

Address

Home	Mobile
Work	Email
Anniversary	Birthday
Notes	

Name

Address

Home	Mobile
Work	Email
Anniversary	Birthday
Notes	

R

Name

Address

Home   Mobile

Work   Email

Anniversary   Birthday

Notes

Name

Address

Home   Mobile

Work   Email

Anniversary   Birthday

Notes

Name

Address

Home   Mobile

Work   Email

Anniversary   Birthday

Notes

R

Name	
Address	

Home	Mobile
Work	Email
Anniversary	Birthday
Notes	

Name	
Address	

Home	Mobile
Work	Email
Anniversary	Birthday
Notes	

Name	
Address	

Home	Mobile
Work	Email
Anniversary	Birthday
Notes	

R

Name

Address

Home | Mobile
Work | Email
Anniversary | Birthday
Notes

Name

Address

Home | Mobile
Work | Email
Anniversary | Birthday
Notes

Name

Address

Home | Mobile
Work | Email
Anniversary | Birthday
Notes

S

Name

Address

Home	Mobile
Work	Email
Anniversary	Birthday
Notes	

Name

Address

Home	Mobile
Work	Email
Anniversary	Birthday
Notes	

Name

Address

Home	Mobile
Work	Email
Anniversary	Birthday
Notes	

Name

Address

Home   Mobile

Work   Email

Anniversary   Birthday

Notes

Name

Address

Home   Mobile

Work   Email

Anniversary   Birthday

Notes

Name

Address

Home   Mobile

Work   Email

Anniversary   Birthday

Notes

S

Name

Address

Home | Mobile
Work | Email
Anniversary | Birthday

Notes

Name

Address

Home | Mobile
Work | Email
Anniversary | Birthday

Notes

Name

Address

Home | Mobile
Work | Email
Anniversary | Birthday

Notes

S

Name

Address

Home   Mobile

Work   Email

Anniversary   Birthday

Notes

Name

Address

Home   Mobile

Work   Email

Anniversary   Birthday

Notes

Name

Address

Home   Mobile

Work   Email

Anniversary   Birthday

Notes

T

Name

Address

Home	Mobile
Work	Email
Anniversary	Birthday

Notes

Name

Address

Home	Mobile
Work	Email
Anniversary	Birthday

Notes

Name

Address

Home	Mobile
Work	Email
Anniversary	Birthday

Notes

Name

Address

Home   Mobile

Work   Email

Anniversary   Birthday

Notes

Name

Address

Home   Mobile

Work   Email

Anniversary   Birthday

Notes

Name

Address

Home   Mobile

Work   Email

Anniversary   Birthday

Notes

T

Name

Address

Home | Mobile
Work | Email
Anniversary | Birthday
Notes

Name

Address

Home | Mobile
Work | Email
Anniversary | Birthday
Notes

Name

Address

Home | Mobile
Work | Email
Anniversary | Birthday
Notes

T

Name

Address

Home	Mobile
Work	Email
Anniversary	Birthday
Notes	

Name

Address

Home	Mobile
Work	Email
Anniversary	Birthday
Notes	

Name

Address

Home	Mobile
Work	Email
Anniversary	Birthday
Notes	

Name

Address

Home   Mobile

Work   Email

Anniversary   Birthday

Notes

Name

Address

Home   Mobile

Work   Email

Anniversary   Birthday

Notes

Name

Address

Home   Mobile

Work   Email

Anniversary   Birthday

Notes

Name

Address

Home   Mobile

Work   Email

Anniversary   Birthday

Notes

Name

Address

Home   Mobile

Work   Email

Anniversary   Birthday

Notes

Name

Address

Home   Mobile

Work   Email

Anniversary   Birthday

Notes

Name

Address

Home   Mobile

Work   Email

Anniversary   Birthday

Notes

Name

Address

Home   Mobile

Work   Email

Anniversary   Birthday

Notes

Name

Address

Home   Mobile

Work   Email

Anniversary   Birthday

Notes

U

Name

Address

Home	Mobile
Work	Email
Anniversary	Birthday

Notes

Name

Address

Home	Mobile
Work	Email
Anniversary	Birthday

Notes

Name

Address

Home	Mobile
Work	Email
Anniversary	Birthday

Notes

Name

Address

Home | Mobile

Work | Email

Anniversary | Birthday

Notes

Name

Address

Home | Mobile

Work | Email

Anniversary | Birthday

Notes

Name

Address

Home | Mobile

Work | Email

Anniversary | Birthday

Notes

Name

Address

Home   Mobile

Work   Email

Anniversary   Birthday

Notes

Name

Address

Home   Mobile

Work   Email

Anniversary   Birthday

Notes

Name

Address

Home   Mobile

Work   Email

Anniversary   Birthday

Notes

V

Name

Address

Home	Mobile
Work	Email
Anniversary	Birthday
Notes	

Name

Address

Home	Mobile
Work	Email
Anniversary	Birthday
Notes	

Name

Address

Home	Mobile
Work	Email
Anniversary	Birthday
Notes	

Name

Address

Home	Mobile
Work	Email
Anniversary	Birthday
Notes	

Name

Address

Home	Mobile
Work	Email
Anniversary	Birthday
Notes	

Name

Address

Home	Mobile
Work	Email
Anniversary	Birthday
Notes	

Name

Address

Home   Mobile

Work   Email

Anniversary   Birthday

Notes

Name

Address

Home   Mobile

Work   Email

Anniversary   Birthday

Notes

Name

Address

Home   Mobile

Work   Email

Anniversary   Birthday

Notes

W

Name	
Address	
Home	Mobile
Work	Email
Anniversary	Birthday
Notes	

Name	
Address	
Home	Mobile
Work	Email
Anniversary	Birthday
Notes	

Name	
Address	
Home	Mobile
Work	Email
Anniversary	Birthday
Notes	

Name

Address

Home   Mobile

Work   Email

Anniversary   Birthday

Notes

Name

Address

Home   Mobile

Work   Email

Anniversary   Birthday

Notes

Name

Address

Home   Mobile

Work   Email

Anniversary   Birthday

Notes

Name

Address

Home | Mobile

Work | Email

Anniversary | Birthday

Notes

Name

Address

Home | Mobile

Work | Email

Anniversary | Birthday

Notes

Name

Address

Home | Mobile

Work | Email

Anniversary | Birthday

Notes

Name	
Address	

Home	Mobile
Work	Email
Anniversary	Birthday
Notes	

Name	
Address	

Home	Mobile
Work	Email
Anniversary	Birthday
Notes	

Name	
Address	

Home	Mobile
Work	Email
Anniversary	Birthday
Notes	

X

Name

Address

Home   Mobile

Work   Email

Anniversary   Birthday

Notes

Name

Address

Home   Mobile

Work   Email

Anniversary   Birthday

Notes

Name

Address

Home   Mobile

Work   Email

Anniversary   Birthday

Notes

Name	
Address	
Home	Mobile
Work	Email
Anniversary	Birthday
Notes	

Name	
Address	
Home	Mobile
Work	Email
Anniversary	Birthday
Notes	

Name	
Address	
Home	Mobile
Work	Email
Anniversary	Birthday
Notes	

Name

Address

Home   Mobile

Work   Email

Anniversary   Birthday

Notes

Name

Address

Home   Mobile

Work   Email

Anniversary   Birthday

Notes

Name

Address

Home   Mobile

Work   Email

Anniversary   Birthday

Notes

Name

Address

Home   Mobile

Work   Email

Anniversary   Birthday

Notes

Name

Address

Home   Mobile

Work   Email

Anniversary   Birthday

Notes

Name

Address

Home   Mobile

Work   Email

Anniversary   Birthday

Notes

Y

Name

Address

Home	Mobile
Work	Email
Anniversary	Birthday
Notes	

Name

Address

Home	Mobile
Work	Email
Anniversary	Birthday
Notes	

Name

Address

Home	Mobile
Work	Email
Anniversary	Birthday
Notes	

Name	
Address	
Home	Mobile
Work	Email
Anniversary	Birthday
Notes	

Name	
Address	
Home	Mobile
Work	Email
Anniversary	Birthday
Notes	

Name	
Address	
Home	Mobile
Work	Email
Anniversary	Birthday
Notes	

Y

Name

Address

Home   Mobile

Work   Email

Anniversary   Birthday

Notes

Name

Address

Home   Mobile

Work   Email

Anniversary   Birthday

Notes

Name

Address

Home   Mobile

Work   Email

Anniversary   Birthday

Notes

Z

Name

Address

Home	Mobile
Work	Email
Anniversary	Birthday

Notes

Name

Address

Home	Mobile
Work	Email
Anniversary	Birthday

Notes

Name

Address

Home	Mobile
Work	Email
Anniversary	Birthday

Notes

Z

Name

Address

Home	Mobile
Work	Email
Anniversary	Birthday
Notes	

Name

Address

Home	Mobile
Work	Email
Anniversary	Birthday
Notes	

Name

Address

Home	Mobile
Work	Email
Anniversary	Birthday
Notes	

Z

Name

Address

Home | Mobile

Work | Email

Anniversary | Birthday

Notes

Name

Address

Home | Mobile

Work | Email

Anniversary | Birthday

Notes

Name

Address

Home | Mobile

Work | Email

Anniversary | Birthday

Notes

Z

Name

Address

Home   Mobile

Work   Email

Anniversary   Birthday

Notes

Name

Address

Home   Mobile

Work   Email

Anniversary   Birthday

Notes

Name

Address

Home   Mobile

Work   Email

Anniversary   Birthday

Notes

NOTES

NOTES

NOTES

Made in the USA
Monee, IL
22 March 2022

93332149R00061